TABLE DES MATIÈRES

Foreword	1
Chapter 1: Introduction to Qi Gong	3
What is Qi Gong? Origins and Philosophy	4
The Foundational Principles of Qi Gong	6
Health and Mind Benefits	8
Qi Gong and Traditional Chinese Medicine	10
Chapter 2: Preparations for Practice	12
Setting Up Your Practice Space	13
Recommended Gear and Attire	15
Mindset and Attitudes for Qi Gong	17
Understanding Qi (Vital Energy)	19
Chapter 3: Foundational Techniques	21
Body Postures and Alignments	22
Fundamental Breathing Techniques	24
Initial Movements and Their Significance	26
Cultivating Inner Balance and Harmony	28
Chapter 4: Beginner Sequences	30

Simple Routines to Get Started	31
Coordinating Breath and Movements	33
Qi Gong for Relaxation and Stress Reduction	35
Tips for Self-Directed Practice	37
Chapter 5: Advanced Refinement of Techniques	40
Developing Awareness of Qi	41
Advanced Breathing Techniques	43
Fluid and Continuous Movements	45
Meditation in Motion	47
Chapter 6: Qi Gong and Daily Wellbeing	49
Integrating Qi Gong into the Daily Routine	50
Qi Gong for Physical Health	52
Balancing Emotions with Qi Gong	54
Qi Gong for Mental Well-being	56
Chapter 7: Variations and Styles of Qi Gong	58
Exploring Different Styles	59
Medical and Therapeutic Qi Gong	61
Martial Qi Gong: Fundamentals and Applications	63
Spiritual Qi Gong: Connection and Enlightenment	65
Chapter 8: Nutrition and Qi Gong	67
Complementary Body Practices	69
The Synergy of Qi Gong and Meditation	71

Expanding Your Practice with Tai Chi	73
Chapter 9: Overcoming Beginner Challenges	75
Establishing a Regular Practice	77
Assessing and Deepening Your Practice	79
The Path of Mastery	81
Chapter 10: A Summary of the Benefits of Qi Gong	83
Continuing the Journey in Qi Gong	85
Inspirations and Tips for Continuing	87
Qi Gong: A Journey of Life	89
Epilogue	91

FOREWORD

QI GONG: A PATH TO INNER HARMONY

✢ ✢ ✢

In this foreword, we open the door to the captivating world of Qi Gong, an ancient Chinese art form that combines movement, breath and meditation to promote balance and harmony between the body and mind. This book, "Qi Gong: Harmony of Body and Mind", is designed as a comprehensive guide for those seeking to explore this transformative practice, whether you are a beginner or an advanced practitioner.

Throughout its pages, we journey into the origins and philosophy of Qi Gong, delving into the roots of this millenary practice and its integration into traditional Chinese medicine. We then embark on exploring the foundational principles of Qi Gong, unlocking the secrets of its effectiveness for physical, emotional and spiritual health.

The heart of this book is dedicated to the practical learning of Qi Gong. You will find detailed instructions for setting up your practice space, choosing your gear and attire, and guidance on cultivating the mindset and attitudes conducive to an effective practice. The following chapters are dedicated to foundational techniques, beginner sequences and advanced refinement of techniques, allowing each individual to progress at their own pace and according to their needs.

We also explore how Qi Gong can be integrated into your daily routine for optimal physical health, emotional balance and mental wellbeing. Additionally, the book provides insights into the different variations and styles of Qi Gong, as well as complementary practices like nutrition, meditation and Tai Chi.

As you navigate the challenges and advancements in your practice, this guide provides practical advice on overcoming difficulties and establishing a regular practice, all the while inviting you to continue your Qi Gong journey with inspiration and guidance for your daily life.

Ultimately, "Qi Gong: Harmony of Body and Mind" is more than just a manual; it is an invitation to embark on a lifelong journey. This journey of self-discovery and inner harmony is accessible to all, and this book aspires to be your steadfast companion along the way.

Welcome to the world of Qi Gong, where every movement, every breath and every moment of meditation brings you closer to a perfect balance between your body and mind.

CHAPTER 1: INTRODUCTION TO QI GONG

WHAT IS QI GONG? ORIGINS AND PHILOSOPHY

✻ ✻ ✻

Qi Gong, an ancient and revered practice, stands as a treasure of Chinese culture. At the crossroads of martial art, meditation and therapeutic exercise, Qi Gong, literally translated as "mastery of vital energy", constitutes an essential component of traditional Chinese medicine.

The origins of Qi Gong date back several millennia, shaping its philosophy and practices throughout the dynasties. Initially developed to enhance health and prolong life, it gradually became infused with Taoist and Buddhist spirituality, evolving into a quest for harmony between man, nature and the universe.

Qi Gong is built on the notion that Qi, or vital energy, circulates in the body along precise pathways called meridians. Health, according to this perspective, depends on the free flow and balance of Qi. Qi Gong practices, therefore, aim at cultivating, regulating and harmonizing this energy throughout the body.

The exercises in Qi Gong, often gentle and meditative, involve fluid motions, static postures, controlled breathing techniques and mental focus. These practices seek not only to improve physical condition but also to balance the mind and emotions, reflecting the holistic Chinese philosophy.

In essence, Qi Gong is not merely a physical exercise; it is a path towards a deeper understanding of oneself and the universe, guided by millennia of wisdom and tradition.

THE FOUNDATIONAL PRINCIPLES OF QI GONG

❋ ❋ ❋

Qi Gong rests upon fundamental principles that guide its practice and philosophy. These principles, rooted in Chinese tradition and wisdom, are essential to understanding and effectively practicing Qi Gong.

1. Harmony of Qi: At the core of Qi Gong lies the concept of Qi, the vital energy that flows within the body. The first foundational principle is the pursuit of harmony of Qi, which entails a smooth and balanced circulation of this energy throughout the body. This harmony is essential in maintaining physical, mental and emotional well-being.

2. Union of Body and Mind: Qi Gong teaches that the body and mind are inherently interconnected. The practice of Qi Gong aims to unify these two aspects of being, allowing for a greater awareness of oneself and a state of overall wellbeing. This principle encourages practitioners to give equal attention to both mental and physical health.

3. Conscious Breathing: Breath is a key element in the practice of Qi Gong. Breathing exercises aim to regulate and deepen respiration, thus promoting improved circulation of Qi. Conscious and controlled breathing also helps to calm the mind and reduce stress.

4. Slowness and Fluidity: Movements in Qi Gong are often slow, fluid and performed with great attention. This slowness allows for a greater awareness of the body and its sensations, while encouraging precision and control. The fluidity of movements promotes the harmonious flow of Qi.

5. Awareness and Meditation: The practice of Qi Gong is not solely physical. It also incorporates a meditative aspect, where awareness and focus play a crucial role. Practitioners are encouraged to maintain a state of mindfulness, allowing for a deeper connection with their bodies and minds.

By integrating these foundational principles into their practice, Qi Gong practitioners can hope to achieve a state of balance and harmony, not only in their practice but also in their daily lives.

HEALTH AND MIND BENEFITS

✼ ✼ ✼

Qi Gong, as a holistic practice, offers a multitude of benefits for physical and mental health. Its beneficial effects, recognized both in traditional Chinese medicine and through modern scientific studies, make it a practice of choice for those seeking to improve their overall well-being.

1. Enhanced Physical Health: Regular practice of Qi Gong contributes to strengthening the musculoskeletal system, improving flexibility and coordination, and aiding in the prevention of diseases. The gentle and thoughtful movements are particularly beneficial for people of all ages, including the elderly and those in physical rehabilitation.

2. Strengthened Immune System: Qi Gong stimulates the immune system, making the body more resistant to illnesses and infections. This is partly due to the reduction of stress and the improved circulation of Qi, which play a key role in maintaining good health.

3. Reduced Stress and Anxiety: The breathing techniques and meditation practiced in Qi Gong are effective in reducing stress and anxiety. These practices help calm the mind, promote relaxation and can improve the quality of sleep.

4. Emotional Balance: Qi Gong helps balance emotions, allowing for better management of anger, sadness and anxiety. It encourages a more positive and serene attitude towards life, contributing to a state of emotional well-being.

5. Improved Focus and Mental Clarity: The practice of Qi Gong requires and develops focus and presence of mind. These skills, when integrated into daily life, can improve performance in various activities, including work and studies.

6. Profound Connection with oneself: Qi Gong allows for an in-depth exploration of one's body and mind, leading to a better understanding of oneself. This practice can be a powerful tool for personal and spiritual development.

In conclusion, Qi Gong, through its multiple benefits for health and mind, proves to be an enriching practice, offering a path towards holistic well-being and a more balanced life.

QI GONG AND TRADITIONAL CHINESE MEDICINE

✻ ✻ ✻

Qi Gong, as an essential component of Traditional Chinese Medicine (TCM), shares and complements its principles and practices. This symbiotic relationship between Qi Gong and TCM offers a unique perspective on health and well-being, distinct from the Western view of medicine.

1. Qi in Traditional Chinese Medicine: In TCM, Qi is considered the vital energy that animates the body and the universe. Health is seen as a state of balance and harmony of Qi within the body. Qi Gong, through its exercises, aims at optimizing the circulation and balance of this vital energy.

2. Meridians and Acupuncture Points: TCM identifies specific channels, called meridians, through which Qi circulates in the body. Qi Gong practices target these meridians, as well as acupuncture points, to regulate the flow of energy and promote healing.

3. The Five Elements and Qi Gong: The theory of the five elements (wood, fire, earth, metal, water) in TCM is also integrated into Qi Gong. Each element is associated with certain bodily and emotional functions. Qi Gong practices can be adapted to balance these elements in the body, thus promoting health and harmony.

4. Prevention and Treatment of Diseases: Whereas Western medicine often focuses on the treatment of symptoms, TCM and Qi Gong prioritize prevention. By maintaining a regular flow of Qi, Qi Gong helps prevent the onset of imbalances that can lead to diseases.

5. Holism and Personalization: TCM and Qi Gong approach health in a holistic manner, considering the interplay between body, mind and environment. Qi Gong exercises are often personalized according to individual needs, reflecting the personalized approach to health in TCM.

Qi Gong, as an integral practice of TCM, offers a path towards comprehensive health, in harmony with the ancient and time-tested principles of traditional Chinese medicine.

CHAPTER 2: PREPARATIONS FOR PRACTICE

SETTING UP YOUR PRACTICE SPACE

❋ ❋ ❋

Setting up an appropriate space for Qi Gong practice is essential in creating an environment conducive to focus and relaxation. A well-prepared environment can significantly enhance the experience and effectiveness of the practice.

1. Choosing the Space: It is preferable to choose a calm and peaceful place, away from distractions and noise. Whether indoors or outdoors, it is important to feel comfortable and safe in this space.

2. Light and Air Circulation: Good natural lighting and air circulation are important. If you practice indoors, make sure the room is well ventilated. If you practice outdoors, choose a place where you can breathe fresh air.

3. Uncluttered Space: Ensure your practice space is large enough to move around freely. A cluttered environment may restrict your movements and affect your focus.

4. Ambiance: Elements such as soft music, soothing

colors or plants can contribute to creating a serene atmosphere. However, these elements should not distract you from your practice.

5. Accessories: While Qi Gong requires little equipment, some accessories can be useful such as a floor mat for comfort or a timer to measure practice time.

A well-set-up space for Qi Gong practice is a sanctuary where body and mind can harmonize, facilitating a deeper and more meaningful practice experience.

RECOMMENDED GEAR AND ATTIRE

❋ ❋ ❋

For practicing Qi Gong, it is important to choose appropriate gear and attire that promote comfort, freedom of movement and alignment with the principles of the discipline.

1. Practice Attire: The ideal attire for Qi Gong is comfortable, loose-fitting and allows for complete freedom of movement. Clothing should not hinder circulation or restrict movements. Natural fabrics such as cotton or linen are preferable as they allow the skin to breathe.

2. Footwear: Qi Gong can be practiced barefoot for better connection with the ground. However, in certain conditions, specific Qi Gong shoes or soft slippers can be used to protect the feet and provide sufficient grip.

3. Accessories: Although Qi Gong does not require much equipment, certain accessories can be useful. For example, a yoga mat can provide comfortable support for floor exercises. A meditation cushion or bench can also be used for seated practices.

4. Practice Environment: While not strictly gear, creating a suitable practice environment, as discussed earlier, is essential. This may include elements such as soft music, dim lighting or objects that promote serenity.

5. Supplementary Gear: For those wishing to deepen their practice, equipment such as Qi Gong balls or sticks can be incorporated. However, these tools are generally not necessary for beginners.

By choosing appropriate attire and gear, you ensure that your Qi Gong practice is as comfortable and effective as possible, allowing for better focus on movements and breathing.

MINDSET AND ATTITUDES FOR QI GONG

✻ ✻ ✻

The mindset and attitudes adopted during Qi Gong practice play a crucial role in the effectiveness and benefits of this discipline. Cultivating the right mentality can greatly enrich the Qi Gong experience and maximize its benefits.

1. Presence and Awareness: Qi Gong practice requires full awareness of the present moment. It is essential to focus on the present moment, letting go of everyday worries and distractions. This presence of mind fosters a deeper connection with the body and mind.

2. Patience and Perseverance: As with any practice, Qi Gong requires patience. Progress may be slow and subtle. It is important to adopt an attitude of perseverance, remembering that every small improvement contributes to overall well-being.

3. Openness and Acceptance: Qi Gong encourages

an attitude of openness and acceptance. It is important to accept where you are in your practice and in your personal journey. This acceptance allows for practicing without judgment and with kindness towards oneself.

4. Respect for the Body: Listening to and respecting your body is fundamental. This means practicing at a level that is comfortable and pain-free, acknowledging your body's limits and capabilities in each session.

5. Positive Intention: Approaching each Qi Gong session with a positive intention can positively influence the practice. Whether it is for health, emotional balance or peace of mind, keeping this intention in mind can help direct energy and focus.

6. Harmony and Balance: Qi Gong aims to cultivate harmony and balance, not only in the practice itself but also in daily life. Seeking to integrate these principles outside of Qi Gong sessions can lead to a more balanced and serene life experience.

By cultivating an appropriate mindset and attitudes, the practice of Qi Gong becomes not merely a physical and energetic exercise, but also a path towards greater inner peace and harmony with the world around us.

UNDERSTANDING QI (VITAL ENERGY)

✻ ✻ ✻

Qi, often translated as "vital energy", is a central concept in the practice of Qi Gong and in traditional Chinese medicine. Understanding Qi is essential to grasping the foundations of Qi Gong and to practicing effectively.

1. Definition of Qi: In Chinese philosophy, Qi represents the vital energy that flows in the universe and in the human body. It is considered the life force that maintains balance and animates life.

2. Qi in the Body: According to traditional Chinese medicine, Qi circulates in the body through channels called meridians. A balanced and flowing Qi is synonymous with health and well-being, while imbalances or blockages of Qi can lead to illness.

3. Types of Qi: There are several types of Qi in the body, including acquired Qi, which comes from food and air, and ancestral Qi, which is inherited at birth. Each plays a different role in maintaining health.

4. Cultivating and Regulating Qi: The practice of Qi

Gong aims to cultivate, regulate and harmonize Qi. Through specific movements, breathing techniques and meditation, Qi Gong helps to improve the circulation of Qi and to remove blockages.

5. Qi Gong and Health: By working with Qi, Qi Gong can have beneficial effects on physical and mental health. It helps to strengthen the immune system, reduce stress, improve flexibility and strength, and promote a state of emotional balance.

6. Sensitivity to Qi: With regular practice, Qi Gong practitioners can become more sensitive to their own Qi and to that which surrounds them. This heightened sensitivity allows for greater awareness of their state of health and their environment.

Understanding and working with Qi is a journey of personal discovery and transformation. Qi Gong, as a practice dedicated to the mastery of this vital energy, offers a path towards holistic health and profound well-being.

CHAPTER 3: FOUNDATIONAL TECHNIQUES

BODY POSTURES AND ALIGNMENTS

✳ ✳ ✳

Postures and body alignments are fundamental in the practice of Qi Gong. They constitute the foundation upon which the entire discipline rests, influencing the circulation of Qi and the effectiveness of movements. Proper posture and correct alignment are essential for deriving the maximum benefits from the practice.

1. Standing Posture: The basic standing posture in Qi Gong is often a standing position, with feet parallel and hip-width apart. The knees are slightly bent, the pelvis neutral, and the spine upright yet relaxed. This posture favors good circulation of Qi.

2. Spinal Alignment: Correct alignment of the spine is crucial. Imagine a thread pulling the crown of your head towards the sky, thus elongating the spine while allowing other parts of the body to remain relaxed. This alignment helps maintain balance and facilitates the flow of Qi.

3. Relaxation of Shoulders and Neck: The shoulders

should be relaxed and down, and the neck should be relaxed. This relaxation helps avoid muscle tension and promotes better circulation of energy.

4. Position of Hands and Arms: In many postures, the hands and arms are used to guide and control the movement of Qi. They should be held in a supple and natural manner, without rigidity or excessive tension.

5. Body Awareness: Being aware of your body and its posture is essential. This awareness helps correct imbalances and refine positions for better practice.

6. Stability and Grounding: The practice of Qi Gong requires a sense of grounding, as if the feet were firmly anchored to the ground. This helps with stability and the rooting of energy.

By mastering body postures and alignment, Qi Gong practitioners can improve the circulation of Qi, increase their balance and stability, and deepen their practice.

FUNDAMENTAL BREATHING TECHNIQUES

✻ ✻ ✻

Breathing is a central element in the practice of Qi Gong. It plays a crucial role in regulating Qi (vital energy) and influences both physical and mental health. The fundamental breathing techniques of Qi Gong are designed to improve the circulation of energy and to promote relaxation and focus.

1. Abdominal Breathing: Abdominal breathing is a basic technique where you breathe deeply using the diaphragm. During inhalation, the abdomen expands, and during exhalation, it contracts. This method improves the oxygenation of the blood and promotes relaxation.

2. Conscious Breathing: This technique involves being fully aware of each breath, focusing on the flow of air going in and out of the body. It helps calm the mind and focus on the present moment.

3. Coordination of Breathing and Movement: In

Qi Gong, movements are often coordinated with the breath. For example, one inhales while opening the arms and exhales while closing them. This synchronization enhances the effect of the exercises on Qi.

4. Complete Breathing: This technique combines abdominal and thoracic breathing, allowing for a deeper inhalation and better circulation of energy. It is particularly beneficial for strengthening the lungs and revitalizing the body.

5. Breathing for Qi Circulation: Certain breathing techniques are specifically designed to direct Qi through the meridians and internal organs. These techniques can be more advanced and often require the guidance of an experienced instructor.

6. Regular Practice: The key to mastering breathing techniques is regular practice. It not only allows for improving the technique but also for integrating conscious breathing into daily life for overall well-being.

By incorporating these fundamental breathing techniques into your daily Qi Gong practice, you can significantly improve your health, your energy balance and your state of mental and emotional well-being.

INITIAL MOVEMENTS AND THEIR SIGNIFICANCE

✽ ✽ ✽

In Qi Gong, the initial movements serve as the foundation for the practice and hold deep significance. These movements are designed to prepare the body and mind for the session, while initiating the circulation of Qi (vital energy). Understanding their significance enriches the practice and deepens the experience.

1. Opening and Closing the Arms: This basic movement involves opening the arms laterally and bringing them back in front of the body. It symbolizes the acceptance and reception of energy from the universe, followed by the integration of this energy into the body.

2. Raising and Lowering the Hands: This gesture involves raising the hands in front of oneself and slowly lowering them. It represents the connection between heaven (Yin) and earth (Yang) and promotes the balance of energies in the body.

3. Rotation of the Waist: The gentle rotation of the waist while keeping the arms relaxed helps release tension in the lower back. This movement symbolizes flexibility and fluidity, essential for the harmonious circulation of Qi.

4. Swaying: Swaying back and forth or side to side helps relax the body and release tensions. It represents the natural movement of life and the ability to adapt to changes.

5. Tapping or Patting: Light tapping on different parts of the body stimulates the meridians and acupuncture points. This movement helps awaken the body and prepare the energy channels for the practice.

6. Coordinated Breaths: Each movement in Qi Gong is often accompanied by a conscious breath, reinforcing the unity of body and mind and the focus on the present moment.

Regular practice of these initial movements prepares the body and mind for more advanced exercises, while fostering a deeper understanding of the philosophy and principles of Qi Gong.

CULTIVATING INNER BALANCE AND HARMONY

✹ ✹ ✹

The practice of Qi Gong aims to cultivate an inner balance and harmony, essential for overall health and well-being. This quest for balance is achieved through the integration of mind, body and vital energy (Qi).

1. Yin-Yang Balance: Qi Gong is based on the principle of Yin and Yang, opposing yet complementary forces. The practice seeks to balance these forces within the body, thus promoting health and emotional stability.

2. Body-Mind Harmonization: Qi Gong emphasizes the unity of body and mind. Through meditation and conscious movements, it helps align thoughts, emotions and actions, leading to a state of clarity and inner calm.

3. Stress and Emotion Management: The breathing techniques and meditation in Qi Gong are effective in managing stress and balancing emotions. By practicing regularly, one learns to stay centered and calm, even in stressful situations.

4. Qi Circulation and Balancing: The practice of Qi Gong aims to ensure a smooth circulation of Qi through the meridians. Proper circulation of Qi is associated with robust health and a sharp mind.

5. Enhanced Intuition and Awareness: By cultivating inner harmony, practitioners develop an increased sensitivity to their intuition and a deeper awareness of their inner being and their environment.

6. Regular and Intentional Practice: The key to achieving balance and harmony is regular and intentional practice. Each session should be approached with an open mind and a heart ready to receive and learn.

Ultimately, Qi Gong offers a path towards inner balance and harmony, which proves to be a constant journey of self-exploration and personal transformation.

CHAPTER 4: BEGINNER SEQUENCES

SIMPLE ROUTINES TO GET STARTED

✣ ✣ ✣

For beginners in Qi Gong, it is essential to start with simple routines that allow for a gradual initiation into the practice. These routines are designed to be accessible while providing a solid introduction to the fundamental principles of Qi Gong.

1. Gentle Warm-up: Begin with warm-up exercises to relax the body and mind. This may include light stretching, joint rotations and gentle movements to prepare the body for the practice.

2. Basic Movements: Integrate basic movements such as opening and closing the arms, gentle body bends, and waist rotations. These movements help familiarize the body with the energy flows of Qi Gong.

3. Focus on Breathing: Pay particular attention to breathing. Practice deep abdominal breathing and coordinate your breath with each movement, to harmonize body and mind.

4. Standing Qi Gong Exercises: Standing postures,

such as "the Tree" or "Holding the Ball", are excellent for beginners. They help develop stability, balance and focus.

5. Fluid and Continuous Movements: Practice fluid and continuous movements to promote the circulation of Qi. Avoid abrupt or jerky movements to maintain a gentle and steady practice.

6. Short Sequences: Start with short and simple sequences, gradually adding more movements and increasing the duration of the practice.

Simple routines for beginners are fundamental in building a solid foundation in the practice of Qi Gong. They pave the way for deeper exploration and a more profound engagement with this ancient discipline.

COORDINATING BREATH AND MOVEMENTS

* * *

Coordinating the breath with movements is an essential aspect of Qi Gong, contributing to the fluidity and effectiveness of the practice. This harmonization strengthens the connection between body and mind, and maximizes the circulation of Qi (vital energy).

1. Basic Synchronization: The basic rule is to inhale during opening or expanding movements and exhale during closing or contracting movements. This synchronization helps integrate body and mind into a unified movement.

2. Fluidity of Movements: Coordinated breathing makes movements more fluid and natural. It helps avoid rigidity and tension, promoting a more relaxed and effective practice.

3. Enhanced Focus: Focusing on the breath helps focus the mind, pushing away distractions and promoting a full and present experience in the exercise.

4. Energy Management: Breathing plays a key role in energy management. Inhaling can be seen as drawing energy towards oneself, while exhaling helps dispel stress and negative energies.

5. Deepening of the Practice: With time and practice, the coordination between breath and movements becomes more intuitive and can lead to deeper meditative states.

6. Tips for Beginners: If you are a beginner, start with simple exercises to get used to this coordination. Do not worry if it feels challenging at first; it will become more natural with practice.

By regularly practicing the coordination of breath and movements, Qi Gong practitioners can experience greater harmony and balance in their practice, which positively translates into their daily lives.

QI GONG FOR RELAXATION AND STRESS REDUCTION

✻ ✻ ✻

Qi Gong is particularly effective for relaxation and stress reduction. Through its breathing techniques, movement and meditation, it offers a powerful way to calm the mind and relax the body, thus contributing to better stress management in everyday life.

1. Deep Relaxation: The slow and fluid movements of Qi Gong promote deep relaxation of the body. By focusing on gentle movements, the practitioner can release physical and mental tensions.

2. Conscious Breathing: Breath is a powerful tool for calming the mind. Deep breathing techniques help reduce stress levels and improve mental clarity.

3. Meditation in Motion: Qi Gong is often described as a form of meditation in motion. This practice allows one to focus on the present moment, thus distancing anxious thoughts and worries.

4. Emotional Balance: By regulating the flow of energy in the body, Qi Gong can help balance emotions, reducing feelings of stress, anxiety, and depression.

5. Improved Sleep: Regular practice of Qi Gong can improve the quality of sleep. A calm mind and a relaxed body are essential for restful sleep.

6. Tips for Practice: For relaxation and stress reduction, favor gentle sequences and breathing exercises. Practice in a calm and comfortable environment and try to maintain a regularity in your practice.

By integrating Qi Gong into your daily routine, you can develop effective tools to manage stress and promote a state of overall wellbeing. This can not only improve your quality of life but also increase your capacity to face daily challenges.

TIPS FOR SELF-DIRECTED PRACTICE

❊ ❊ ❊

Developing self-direction in the practice of Qi Gong is a key element for progress and to fully benefit from the rewards of this discipline. Here are some tips to encourage self-direction and enhance your personal practice.

1. Establish a Daily Routine: Regularity is essential. Try to practice at the same time each day to establish a routine. Even a few minutes a day can have a significant impact.

2. Create a Personal Practice Space: As mentioned earlier, having a dedicated space for practice can enhance your focus and commitment to Qi Gong.

3. Listen to Your Body: Learn to listen to and respond to your body's needs. Adapt your practice according to your health condition, energy level, and physical limitations.

4. Keep a Practice Journal: Documenting your experiences, progress, and challenges can help you better understand your journey and adjust your practice accordingly.

5. Set Achievable Goals: Define clear and achievable goals for your Qi Gong practice. This may include aspects such as duration of practice, learning new routines, or improving breathing technique.

6. Explore Diverse Styles and Techniques: Do not limit yourself to a single method. Experiment with different styles and techniques of Qi Gong to enrich your practice and find what suits you best.

7. Use Educational Resources: Books, online videos, and workshops can be excellent resources to deepen your understanding and practice of Qi Gong.

8. Join a Community: While self-direction is important, joining a Qi Gong community can provide support, inspiration, and learning opportunities.

9. Reflection and Introspection: Take time after each session to reflect on your practice. What did you feel? What were the challenges and successes?

10. Stay Open to Learning: Qi Gong is a journey of continuous discovery. Stay open to learning and evolving your practice.

By following these tips, you can become more self-

directed in your Qi Gong practice, which will allow you to fully enjoy the many health and well-being benefits of this ancient discipline.

CHAPTER 5: ADVANCED REFINEMENT OF TECHNIQUES

DEVELOPING AWARENESS OF QI

✻ ✻ ✻

Deepening the practice of Qi Gong involves developing an increased awareness of Qi, the vital energy circulating in the body. This awareness is crucial for improving the mastery of Qi circulation and enhancing the benefits of the practice.

1. Sensitization to Qi: Begin with exercises aimed at feeling Qi in your hands and body. Techniques such as Qi Gong energy balls can help develop this sensitivity.

2. Focused Meditation: Use meditation to focus your mind on different parts of your body. Imagine the flow of Qi moving through the meridians, nourishing each organ.

3. Regular Practice: Regularity is essential for developing a deeper awareness of Qi. Integrate daily sessions, even short ones, to maintain and increase this sensitivity.

4. Grounding Exercises: Practices such as the tree pose or standing meditation help strengthen grounding and connection to the Earth, thus increasing the perception of Qi.

5. Visualization: Visualization is a powerful tool in Qi Gong. Visualize Qi flowing freely through your body, clearing blockages and bringing vitality and wellbeing.

6. Inner Listening: Learn to listen to the signals of your body. Recognizing subtle sensations such as warmth, tingling, or lightness can be an indicator of Qi movement.

Developing an awareness of Qi allows for a deeper understanding of the practice of Qi Gong and leads to a richer and more connected experience, both physically and spiritually.

ADVANCED BREATHING TECHNIQUES

❊ ❊ ❊

In the deepening of Qi Gong practice, advanced breathing techniques play a crucial role. These methods allow for greater control and direction of Qi (vital energy), thus enhancing the effects of the exercises on physical and mental health.

1. Reverse Breathing: Unlike abdominal breathing, reverse breathing involves contracting the abdomen during inhalation and relaxing it during exhalation. This technique is often used to strengthen the energy center and increase internal power.

2. Dan Tian Breathing: The Dan Tian, located near the navel, is considered the energy center of the body. Dan Tian breathing focuses on directing Qi into this center during inhalation, and diffusing it throughout the body during exhalation.

3. Embryonic Breathing: This advanced technique aims to minimize external body movements during breathing, creating a deeper and more meditative experience. It is often used for deep calming and intense concentration.

4. Six Sounds Breathing: This method combines breathing with the vocalization of six distinct sounds, each associated with a specific internal organ. It aims to harmonize and purify these organs.

5. Meridian Breathing: This advanced practice involves visualizing Qi moving through specific meridians of the body during breathing. It is used to open energy channels and promote healing.

6. Progressive Practice: These advanced techniques require regular and progressive practice. It is advisable to approach them with caution and ideally under the supervision of a qualified instructor.

Mastering these advanced breathing techniques can significantly enhance your Qi Gong practice, by increasing your mastery of your vital energy and deepening your mind-body connection.

FLUID AND CONTINUOUS MOVEMENTS

* * *

One of the most characteristic and beneficial aspects of Qi Gong is the practice of fluid and continuous movements. This approach not only promotes better circulation of Qi (vital energy) in the body, but also helps to achieve a state of deep relaxation and heightened awareness.

1. **Fluidity of Movements:** In Qi Gong, each movement flows naturally into the next. This fluidity ensures a harmonious circulation of energy, avoiding blockages and tensions.

2. **Slowness and Control:** Movements are performed slowly and with conscious control. This slowness allows for greater internal sensitivity and a better connection with the body.

3. **Coordination with Breathing:** As mentioned earlier, movements are coordinated with the breath. Inhaling during expansion movements and

exhaling during contraction movements reinforces the effect of the exercises.

4. Continuity of Movements: There are no abrupt pauses between movements. Each action ends gently and transitions naturally into the next, creating a constant flow that mirrors the flow of Qi.

5. Regular Practice: Regular practice helps refine the fluidity and continuity of movements. Over time, these movements become more intuitive and more effective.

6. Concentration and Presence: The fluidity of movements helps maintain a centered focus and a presence in the present moment, which is essential for a deep meditative practice.

By regularly practicing fluid and continuous movements, you can improve the circulation of Qi in your body, promote relaxation, and deepen your awareness of your body and mind.

MEDITATION IN MOTION

❋ ❋ ❋

Meditation in motion is a key concept in Qi Gong, combining physical movements with mental focus and conscious breathing. This practice allows for reaching a state of dynamic meditation, where the body and mind are fully engaged in the present moment.

1. Principle of Meditation in Motion: In Qi Gong, meditation is not only a static practice. It involves an active engagement of the body through slow and fluid movements, thus facilitating a dynamic meditative form.

2. Harmony of Movement and Breath: The coordination of breath with movements strengthens concentration and helps guide Qi through the body. This harmonization creates a rhythmic flow that promotes deep relaxation and mental clarity.

3. Focus on the Present Moment: Meditation in motion helps anchor awareness in the present moment. By focusing on each movement and each breath, one releases oneself from distractions and preoccupations of the mind.

4. Health Benefits: This practice offers similar benefits to traditional meditation, such as stress reduction, improved focus, and an overall sense of wellbeing.

5. Accessibility: Meditation in motion is particularly accessible for those who have difficulty remaining still for extended periods. It offers a dynamic alternative to sitting meditation.

6. Integration into Daily Life: The principles of meditation in motion can be integrated into everyday activities. By practicing mindfulness and fluidity in the gestures of daily life, one can experience a form of active meditation throughout the day.

Meditation in motion is an essential component of Qi Gong, offering a path to inner peace and harmony that unifies body, mind, and vital energy.

CHAPTER 6: QI GONG AND DAILY WELLBEING

INTEGRATING QI GONG INTO THE DAILY ROUTINE

* * *

Integrating Qi Gong into the daily routine is an effective way to continuously improve physical and mental health. This regular practice allows to fully benefit from the long-term effects of Qi Gong.

1. Planning Practice Time: Choose a time of the day when you are least likely to be disturbed. This could be in the morning to start the day with energy or in the evening to unwind.

2. Short but Regular Practices: Even short sessions of 10 to 15 minutes can be very beneficial. The key is the regularity of the practice.

3. Integration into Daily Activities: Try to integrate the principles of Qi Gong into your daily activities. Use conscious breathing during stressful situations or practice mindfulness during routine tasks.

4. Using Apps or Guides: Apps or online guides

can help structure your practice and provide guided sessions.

5. Creating a Dedicated Space: If possible, dedicate a space in your home to the practice of Qi Gong. A calm and pleasant environment can greatly enhance the experience.

6. Combining with Other Practices: Qi Gong can be combined with other forms of exercise or meditation for a holistic wellbeing routine.

QI GONG FOR PHYSICAL HEALTH

✽ ✽ ✽

Qi Gong is renowned for its numerous benefits on physical health. This ancient practice involves gentle movements, breathing, and meditation to improve strength, flexibility, and vital functions.

1. Building Strength and Flexibility Qi Gong movements, though gentle, are effective in strengthening muscles, particularly those in the core. They also enhance flexibility and increase joint mobility.

2. Improving Posture Qi Gong exercises involve proper body alignment and balance, aiding in improving posture and reducing pains related to poor posture.

3. Boosting the Circulatory System The combination of movements and breathing techniques promotes better blood circulation, vital for overall health and vitality.

4. Strengthening the Immune System Qi Gong helps stimulate the immune system, increasing the body's resistance to diseases and infections.

5. Pain Management Regular practice of Qi Gong can be effective in managing chronic pain, such as arthritis, fibromyalgia, and back pain.

6. Internal Organ Health Qi Gong exercises also work on internal organs, helping improve their functioning and preventing illnesses.

By incorporating Qi Gong into your daily routine, you can significantly contribute to your physical well-being, promoting a healthier and more balanced way of life.

BALANCING EMOTIONS WITH QI GONG

✾ ✾ ✾

Qi Gong is a deeply transformative practice that can balance emotions and enhance mental health. Through its techniques, it offers a way to effectively manage emotional states and cultivate lasting emotional equilibrium.

1. Releasing Negative Emotions Qi Gong aids in releasing negative emotions such as anxiety, anger, or sadness. The movements and breathing assist in dissolving emotional blockages.

2. Cultivating Positivity By focusing on gentle movements and mindful breathing, Qi Gong fosters positive states of mind, such as serenity and joy.

3. Stress Management Regular Qi Gong practice is an effective means of managing stress, reducing tension, and encouraging relaxation.

4. Enhancing Self-Awareness Qi Gong increases

self-awareness, helping you recognize and understand your inner emotions, which is essential for emotional balance.

5. Specific Breathing Techniques for Emotions Specific breathing techniques can be employed to calm the mind and regulate emotions.

6. Mindfulness Practice The mindfulness incorporated into Qi Gong helps you live in the present moment, reducing excessive preoccupation with the past or future.

By integrating Qi Gong into your life, you can not only improve your physical health but also achieve emotional balance, essential for a fulfilling and healthy life.

QI GONG FOR MENTAL WELL-BEING

* * *

Beyond its physical benefits, Qi Gong also offers considerable advantages for mental well-being. This ancient practice helps reduce stress, improve concentration, and cultivate a profound inner peace.

1. Reducing Stress and Anxiety The breathing and movement techniques of Qi Gong help calm the nervous system, reducing stress and anxiety. With regular practice, you can enter a deeper state of relaxation.

2. Improving Concentration Qi Gong practice requires constant attention and focus, which can improve your ability to concentrate in other areas of life.

3. Boosting Mental Clarity By balancing the Qi in the body, Qi Gong promotes better energy flow to the brain, enhancing mental clarity and cognitive function.

4. Emotional Balance By regulating the energy in the body, Qi Gong helps balance emotions, leading to a more stable state of emotional equilibrium.

5. Building Resilience Regular practice of Qi Gong strengthens mental resilience, helping you better cope with life's challenges and changes.

6. Promoting Mindfulness Qi Gong is a form of moving meditation that encourages living fully in the present moment, increasing self-awareness and presence.

By incorporating Qi Gong into your daily routine, you can not only improve your physical health but also strengthen your mental well-being, essential for a balanced and harmonious life.

CHAPTER 7: VARIATIONS AND STYLES OF QI GONG

EXPLORING DIFFERENT STYLES

✳ ✳ ✳

Qi Gong, with its ancient roots and evolution through centuries, presents a diversity of styles and forms. Each style possesses unique characteristics and specific benefits, offering practitioners a wide array of choices.

1. Medical Qi Gong This style focuses on healing and preventing illnesses. It uses specific movements to target and improve the function of various organs and bodily systems.

2. Martial Qi Gong Associated with Chinese martial arts, this style emphasizes strengthening the body and cultivating internal energy, Qi, for martial performance.

3. Spiritual Qi Gong With roots in Taoism and Buddhism, this style aims for the purification of the mind and the pursuit of spiritual awakening, in addition to physical and mental balance.

4. Contemporary Qi Gong These modern forms of Qi Gong integrate elements of modern medicine and relaxation techniques, making them particularly suited to contemporary lifestyles.

5. Qi Gong for Longevity Focused on slowing the aging process, this style combines gentle exercises and breathing techniques to promote vitality and longevity.

6. Dynamic Qi Gong Involving more vigorous movements and deep breathing exercises, this style is often more energetic and stimulating.

7. Silk Reeling Qi Gong Based on fluid and continuous movements, this style is known for its grace and softness, mimicking the movement of silk.

Exploring different Qi Gong styles can enrich your practice, allowing you to discover the one that resonates most with your personal needs and goals. Each style offers a unique perspective and specific benefits for overall well-being.

MEDICAL AND THERAPEUTIC QI GONG

✤ ✤ ✤

Medical and therapeutic Qi Gong is a specific branch of Qi Gong that focuses on healing and maintaining health. Used as a complement to traditional Chinese medicine, it offers targeted techniques for treating and preventing various ailments.

1. Foundations of Medical Qi Gong This style uses specific exercises to influence the flow of Qi (life energy) in the body, aiming to restore balance and promote healing.

2. Treating Specific Conditions Medical Qi Gong can be tailored to address specific conditions such as hypertension, arthritis, or digestive disorders, depending on individual needs.

3. Health Prevention and Maintenance Beyond treatment, it is also used for disease prevention and general health maintenance, by strengthening the immune system and improving the body's resilience.

4. Breathing and Movement Techniques Practices involve deep breathing techniques, gentle movements, and focused meditations, designed to target specific areas of the body.

5. Integration with Conventional Medicine Medical Qi Gong is often used as a complement to conventional medical treatments, offering a holistic approach to health.

6. Self-Practice for Well-being Practitioners are encouraged to engage in daily self-practice to maximize the health benefits and accelerate the healing process.

Medical and therapeutic Qi Gong is a powerful tool for those seeking to complement their healing journey with a natural and holistic approach, promoting health and well-being on all levels.

MARTIAL QI GONG: FUNDAMENTALS AND APPLICATIONS

※ ※ ※

Martial Qi Gong is a dynamic form of Qi Gong integrated into Chinese martial arts. This style emphasizes the cultivation of internal energy, Qi, for increased strength, endurance, and martial prowess.

1. Origin and Philosophy Martial Qi Gong finds its roots in ancient Chinese martial traditions. It draws upon the principles of traditional Chinese medicine and the harmonization of Yin and Yang.

2. Strengthening Qi This form of Qi Gong aims to accumulate and strengthen Qi within the body, thereby increasing physical strength, vitality, and resistance to injury.

3. Specific Techniques Martial Qi Gong involves dynamic and sometimes vigorous exercises that may include punches, kicks, and other powerful movements, all performed with deep concentration and control.

4. Application in Martial Arts Martial arts practitioners use Qi Gong to enhance their skills, increase their strength, and develop a stronger mental presence during combat.

5. Balance and Control In addition to strength, Martial Qi Gong teaches balance, coordination, and body control, essential elements for any martial artist.

6. Personal Development Beyond its physical applications, Martial Qi Gong also contributes to personal discipline, focus, and self-mastery.

Martial Qi Gong is a powerful practice that offers significant benefits for those engaged in martial arts while also contributing to overall health and well-being.

SPIRITUAL QI GONG: CONNECTION AND ENLIGHTENMENT

* * *

Spiritual Qi Gong is a form of practice that emphasizes the spiritual and energetic aspects of Qi Gong. This style aims to develop a deep inner connection, heightened awareness, and spiritual awakening.

1. **Mind-Body Connection** Spiritual Qi Gong focuses on harmonizing the mind and body, fostering a deeper understanding of oneself and the universe.

2. **Cultivating Awareness** This practice involves inner exploration, helping to awaken higher consciousness and develop intuition and psychic perception.

3. **Meditation and Visualization** Deep meditation techniques and visualization are often used to

facilitate spiritual awakening and the circulation of Qi.

4. Chakra Balancing Some styles of spiritual Qi Gong work on balancing and opening the chakras, the energy centers of the body, for overall balance and harmony.

5. Connection with Nature Spiritual Qi Gong often encourages practicing outdoors, connecting with the natural elements and the energy of the earth and sky.

6. Path to Enlightenment For many practitioners, spiritual Qi Gong is a path toward spiritual enlightenment and greater self-realization.

By practicing spiritual Qi Gong, individuals can explore deeper dimensions of their being, opening the way for personal transformation and a profound connection with the world around them.

CHAPTER 8: NUTRITION AND QI GONG

✽ ✽ ✽

Nutrition plays a crucial role in the practice of Qi Gong, as it contributes to the body's energy balance and overall health. A well-balanced diet can enhance the effectiveness of one's Qi Gong practice and improve general well-being.

1. The Principle of Balanced Nutrition In Qi Gong philosophy, a balanced diet is essential. This involves consuming a variety of foods that nourish the body and support the flow of Qi.

2. Foods and Qi Energy Certain foods are known for their ability to increase Qi energy. These foods include whole grains, green vegetables, fruits, nuts, and seeds.

3. Importance of Fresh Foods Fresh and natural foods are preferred as they contain more Qi. Processed and refined foods are often devoid of this vital energy.

4. Respecting the Seasons Eating in accordance with the seasons and choosing local foods can also contribute to harmony with the natural environment and the cycle of the seasons.

5. Moderation and Mindfulness Eating in moderation and with mindfulness is encouraged in Qi Gong. This means eating until satisfied but not to excess, and being fully present during meals.

6. Combining with Practice A healthy diet combined with regular Qi Gong practice can lead to significant improvements in health and well-being.

By incorporating a healthy and balanced diet into your Qi Gong practice, you can nourish both your body and mind, promoting optimal health and energy balance.

COMPLEMENTARY BODY PRACTICES

※ ※ ※

In addition to Qi Gong, incorporating other body practices can enrich and complement your overall well-being routine. These complementary activities can help enhance the effects of Qi Gong by improving flexibility, strength, and general balance.

1. Yoga Yoga, with its postures (asanas) and breathing techniques (pranayama), is an excellent complementary practice. It shares with Qi Gong the goal of mind-body harmony.

2. Tai Chi Tai Chi, often regarded as a form of Qi Gong, is an internal martial art that emphasizes slow, flowing movements. It is great for improving balance and coordination.

3. Pilates Pilates focuses on core strength, postural alignment, and flexibility. It can be an excellent complement to Qi Gong for developing muscular strength and stability.

4. Mindful Walking Mindful walking, or meditative walking, is a simple yet powerful practice that encourages mindfulness and connection with nature.

5. Stretching Stretching exercises help maintain the body's flexibility, which is beneficial for the movements practiced in Qi Gong.

6. Dance Dance, as a form of body expression, can improve fluidity of movement and emotional expression, complementing the more structured aspects of Qi Gong.

By combining Qi Gong with these body practices, you can create a holistic approach to your well-being, addressing not only physical health but also mental and emotional aspects.

THE SYNERGY OF QI GONG AND MEDITATION

✻ ✻ ✻

Practicing Qi Gong and meditation together creates a powerful synergy, enhancing the benefits of each discipline. This combination offers a holistic approach for the development of body, mind, and vital energy.

1. **Mutual Reinforcement** Qi Gong, with its movements and breathing, prepares the body and mind for meditation, making the meditative experience deeper and more centered.

2. **Circulation of Qi** Qi Gong promotes the circulation of Qi, which can improve the quality of meditation by calming the mind and stabilizing emotions.

3. **Body Awareness** Qi Gong practice develops body awareness, which can be integrated into seated meditation, contributing to better posture and greater physical presence.

4. Depth of Meditation Meditation helps internalize the benefits of Qi Gong, allowing for a deeper understanding of the movements and a stronger connection with internal energy.

5. Stress Management Together, Qi Gong and meditation are effective tools for managing stress and anxiety, offering techniques to calm the mind and relax the body.

6. Daily Practice Integrating short meditation sessions before or after Qi Gong practice can strengthen your daily well-being routine.

Combining Qi Gong and meditation creates a comprehensive practice that nourishes physical, mental, and spiritual balance, leading to enhanced overall health and well-being.

EXPANDING YOUR PRACTICE WITH TAI CHI

❉ ❉ ❉

Tai Chi, often considered a form of Qi Gong, is an ideal complementary practice for those looking to expand their Qi Gong practice. Tai Chi combines flowing, slow movements with deep breathing and mindfulness, offering similar yet distinct benefits.

1. Fluid and Graceful Movements Tai Chi is known for its slow, fluid, and graceful movements that improve balance, coordination, and fluidity of motion.

2. Concentration and Mindfulness Like Qi Gong, Tai Chi encourages concentration and mindfulness, helping to calm the mind and reduce stress.

3. Strength and Flexibility While gentle, Tai Chi is effective in strengthening muscles, improving flexibility, and joint mobility.

4. Meditation in Motion Tai Chi is often described

as meditation in motion, allowing for a deep exploration of the mind-body connection.

5. Complementarity with Qi Gong Practicing Tai Chi can complement and enhance your Qi Gong practice by offering a new dimension to the exploration of Qi (life energy).

6. Accessibility Tai Chi is accessible to all ages and fitness levels, making it ideal for those seeking a gentle yet effective practice.

By integrating Tai Chi into your Qi Gong routine, you can benefit from a more well-rounded holistic approach to your health and well-being, enriching your journey in energy arts.

CHAPTER 9: OVERCOMING BEGINNER CHALLENGES

※ ※ ※

Embarking on a new practice like Qi Gong can present challenges. It is essential to approach these obstacles with patience and persistence to progress and get the most out of your practice.

1. **Unfamiliarity** Initially, the movements and concepts of Qi Gong may seem foreign. Take time to learn gradually and do not get discouraged by the initial complexity.

2. **Concentration Difficulties** The concentration required for Qi Gong can be challenging. Practice in a calm environment and try meditation techniques to improve your focus.

3. **Lack of Coordination** If you struggle with coordinating movements and breathing, start

with simple exercises and gradually increase the complexity.

4. Unrealistic Expectations It is important to have realistic expectations and understand that Qi Gong is a journey. Benefits come with time and regular practice.

5. Maintaining Regularity Regularity is key to progression in Qi Gong. Try to practice a little each day, even for short durations.

6. Seeking Guidance Do not hesitate to seek guidance from a qualified instructor, especially if you feel lost or need advice.

Overcoming these initial challenges can pave the way for a rewarding and transformative experience with Qi Gong, leading to significant improvements in health and well-being.

ESTABLISHING A REGULAR PRACTICE

❋ ❋ ❋

Establishing a regular Qi Gong practice is essential for maximizing its benefits. Consistency is key to deepening your practice and achieving tangible results on physical, mental, and spiritual levels.

1. Setting a Regular Time Choose a time of day that works for you to practice and try to stick to it. Whether it's in the morning for an energetic start or in the evening for deep relaxation, consistency is important.

2. Creating a Dedicated Space Having a dedicated space for your practice can reinforce your commitment. This could be a quiet corner in your home or a spot in nature.

3. Setting Realistic Goals Set achievable goals for your practice. Start with short sessions and gradually increase the duration and complexity as you progress.

4. Gradual Integration Start with short sessions and gradually increase the duration and complexity of your practices.

5. Practice Journal Keeping a journal of your practices can help you track your progress and stay motivated.

6. Variety and Exploration Experiment with different Qi Gong styles and techniques to keep your practice engaging and interesting.

Regularity is more important than the length of each session. With regular practice, you will develop greater proficiency in Qi Gong and a deeper understanding of its benefits.

ASSESSING AND DEEPENING YOUR PRACTICE

✽ ✽ ✽

Assessing and deepening your Qi Gong practice is crucial for continuous growth and reaping the maximum benefits of this ancient discipline.

1. Regular Self-Assessment Take time regularly to reflect on your practice. Assess your progress, challenges faced, and areas you wish to improve.

2. Practice Journal Keeping a journal of your experiences, sensations, and progress can provide valuable insights into your journey in Qi Gong.

3. Setting Clear Goals Define specific goals for your practice. These may include improving flexibility, mastering complex techniques, or deepening your meditation.

4. Attending Workshops or Retreats Joining workshops or retreats can provide an immersive learning environment and help you deepen your understanding and practice of Qi Gong.

5. Seeking Feedback If possible, get feedback from instructors or experienced practitioners. Their guidance can be invaluable for refining your technique and deepening your practice.

6. Exploring New Forms Try different forms or styles of Qi Gong. Each style has something unique to offer and can enrich your overall practice.

7. Integration into Daily Life Find ways to incorporate the principles of Qi Gong into your daily life, not just during formal practice.

By regularly assessing and deepening your Qi Gong practice, you can continue to grow in this discipline, enjoying its numerous benefits for health, emotional balance, and spiritual well-being.

THE PATH OF MASTERY

✳ ✳ ✳

The practice of Qi Gong is an ongoing journey of discovery and mastery. As you deepen your understanding and proficiency in Qi Gong, you open the door to endless personal and spiritual development.

1. Continued Learning Continue to learn, whether through advanced classes, books, workshops, or seminars. There is always more to discover in the practice of Qi Gong.

2. Daily Practice The key to mastery is regular practice. Even a short daily practice can be extremely beneficial.

3. Experimentation and Adaptation Do not be afraid to experiment with different styles and techniques to find what resonates most with you.

4. Teaching and Sharing Teaching or sharing your knowledge with others can enrich your own understanding and practice of Qi Gong.

5. Community Connection Join a Qi Gong community to exchange experiences, learn from others, and feel supported in your practice.

6. Introspection and Reflection Take time for inner reflection. This may involve meditation, journaling, or simply spending time in nature.

7. Balance and Harmony Seek balance in your life – between work, play, Qi Gong practice, and other aspects of your life.

The path of mastery in Qi Gong is a personal and unique journey. Each step forward on this path contributes to greater well-being, improved health, and spiritual fulfillment.

CHAPTER 10: A SUMMARY OF THE BENEFITS OF QI GONG

✻ ✻ ✻

As we conclude this guide to Qi Gong, it is essential to recap the numerous benefits this ancient practice offers, highlighting its profound impact on overall health and well-being.

1. Enhanced Physical Health Qi Gong improves flexibility, strengthens muscles and joints, and increases endurance. It also aids in regulating the cardiovascular, respiratory, and digestive systems.

2. Emotional Balance Practicing Qi Gong helps manage stress, reduces anxiety, and fosters a calm and balanced state of mind.

3. Mental and Spiritual Development Qi Gong strengthens concentration, mental clarity, and encourages spiritual awakening, contributing to a better understanding of oneself and the world.

4. Qi Harmony By improving the circulation of Qi, or life energy, in the body, Qi Gong helps maintain optimal health and prevent illnesses.

5. Longevity and Quality of Life Regular Qi Gong practitioners often report an improved quality of life and an increase in their longevity.

6. Versatility and Accessibility Qi Gong is accessible to everyone, regardless of age or physical condition, making its benefits available to a wide population.

Qi Gong, with its vielfältig advantages, is more than just a physical practice; it is a path to holistic health, emotional balance, and spiritual fulfillment.

CONTINUING THE JOURNEY IN QI GONG

* * *

Qi Gong is not merely a practice but a way of life. By continuing your journey in Qi Gong, you open the door to constant transformation and ever-renewing personal growth.

1. **Lifetime Commitment** View Qi Gong as a lifelong commitment. The more you practice, the deeper the benefits will be on your health and well-being.

2. **Continuous Growth** There is always something new to learn in Qi Gong, whether it is an advanced technique, a new form, or a deeper understanding of its philosophy.

3. **Sharing and Community** Share your Qi Gong experience with others. Joining a community or practice group can offer support and inspiration.

4. **Teaching and Mentorship** Consider teaching Qi Gong or becoming a mentor to others. Teaching is

an excellent way to deepen your own practice and understanding.

5. Integration into Daily Life Find ways to integrate the principles of Qi Gong into your daily life, not just your formal practice.

6. Exploring Traditional Chinese Medicine Deepening your knowledge of traditional Chinese medicine can complement your Qi Gong practice.

7. Maintaining a Curious Mind Stay curious and open to learning. Every step on your journey can bring new perspectives and discoveries.

Qi Gong is a lifelong journey, and each step on this path offers unique opportunities for growth, exploration, and fulfillment.

INSPIRATIONS AND TIPS FOR CONTINUING

✽ ✽ ✽

As we conclude this guide to Qi Gong, it is important to remember that the practice of Qi Gong is an endless journey, rich in discoveries and personal growth. Here are some inspirations and tips to continue on this path with enthusiasm and dedication.

1. Seek Inspiration Find inspiration in the stories of great Qi Gong masters, in nature, art, music, or in the accounts of those who have transformed their lives through this practice.

2. Stay Open and Curious Be open to continuous learning and the exploration of new techniques and philosophies. Curiosity is your best guide on this journey.

3. Create a Personalized Routine Develop a Qi Gong routine that meets your unique needs, adapting to changes in your life and your body.

4. Practice with Joy Approach each Qi Gong session with joy and gratitude. Practice should not be a chore, but a cherished time to connect with yourself.

5. Share Your Experience Share your knowledge and experience with others. Teaching can be a powerful source of inspiration for your own practice.

6. Integrate Qi Gong into Daily Life Find ways to practice the principles of Qi Gong in your日常生活的, such as mindfulness during everyday tasks.

7. Be Patient and Kind to Yourself Recognize that progress can be gradual and that every small step counts. Be patient with yourself on less motivated days.

8. Plan Your Path Think about where you want Qi Gong to take you in the coming years and plan accordingly, whether in terms of health, well-being, or spiritual development.

Qi Gong is a journey of life, a path of constant learning and evolution. By staying true to your practice and exploring new facets of this ancient discipline, you will continue to reap its benefits throughout your life.

QI GONG: A JOURNEY OF LIFE

❋ ❋ ❋

Qi Gong, more than just a physical practice or a healing method, is a path of life. This journey, rich in discoveries and transformations, invites us to explore the depths of our being and establish lasting harmony with the world around us.

1. An Evolutionary Practice Qi Gong is a lifelong companion that evolves with you, adapting to your needs, challenges, and aspirations at every stage of your journey.

2. The Limitless Potential for Growth Each Qi Gong practice is an opportunity to learn and grow. There is no end to what you can discover about yourself and the energy that surrounds you.

3. A Commitment to Self Qi Gong is a commitment to your well-being and fulfillment. It is a promise to care for your body, mind, and spirit.

4. Harmony with Nature and the Universe Qi Gong helps us synchronize with the rhythms of nature and the universe, reminding us that we are an integral part of a larger whole.

5. A Path to Wisdom Beyond physical health and mental balance, Qi Gong is a path to deep wisdom and a richer understanding of life.

6. A Source of Inspiration and Peace Qi Gong can become a constant source of inspiration and inner peace, helping you navigate life with grace and tranquility.

7. Transmission and Sharing As a journey of life, Qi Gong is also a legacy that you can share with others, enriching the lives of those around you.

Qi Gong is more than a practice; it is a way of life, a path to balance and harmony, and a perpetual quest for personal and spiritual fulfillment. Embrace this journey with heart and openness, and discover the infinite treasures it has to offer.

EPILOGUE

QI GONG: A PATH TO INNER HARMONY

As we close our in-depth exploration of Qi Gong, it is time to reflect on the journey we have undertaken together through this book. "Qi Gong: A Path to Inner Harmony" was designed as an open window into an ancient world, inviting each reader to discover, learn, and grow through the practice of Qi Gong.

We have journeyed through the ancient origins of this practice, its fundamental principles, and explored in depth the many ways it can enrich our health and well-being. Each chapter has been a step forward in understanding this art form that balances and harmonizes the body, mind, and life energy.

This book has guided you through the initial stages of preparation, the basic techniques, and accompanied you in the development of your personal practice. We have covered the various styles and variations of Qi Gong, as well as its integration with other complementary practices, emphasizing the importance of synergy between movement, breath, and state of mind.

By presenting you with challenges and ways to overcome obstacles, this guide has sought to inspire a regular and profound practice, encouraging you to view Qi Gong not only as a physical or spiritual activity but as a path of life, a continuous quest for balance and harmony.

As you close this book, you are not merely concluding a chapter of reading but standing at the threshold of a world of endless possibilities. Qi Gong is an endless journey, a constant exploration of oneself and a continuous blossoming. Whether you are at the beginning of your path or well advanced on the way, remember that each practice is an opportunity to discover something new about yourself and the universe that surrounds you.

I invite you to continue your Qi Gong practice with curiosity, open-mindedness, and a joyful heart. May this book be a constant source of inspiration and guidance on your path to inner harmony.

❋ ❋ ❋

Thank you for taking this journey with "Qi Gong: A Path to Inner Harmony." May your practice continue to bring you health, peace, and balance.

Printed in Great Britain
by Amazon